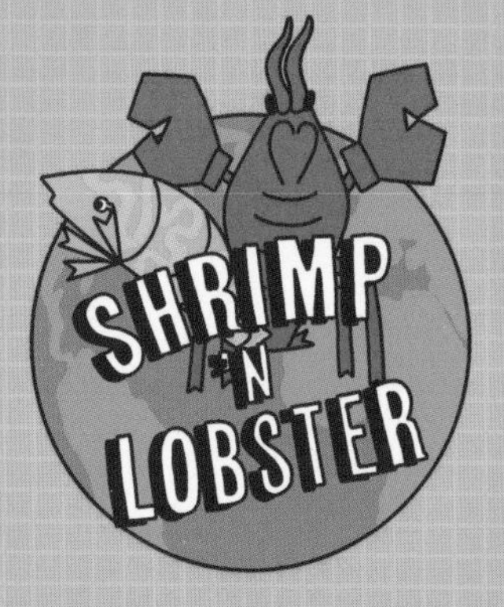

WRITTEN AND
ILLUSTRATED BY
CHARLOTTE RYGH

A SAN FRANCISCO ADVENTURE

Design by Laurie Ormonde and David Miles

The Collective Book Studio®
Oakland, California
www.thecollectivebook.studio

ISBN: 978-1-951412-06-7
LCCN: 2020906127

Manufactured in China

10 9 8 7 6 5 4 3 2

CONTENTS

WELCOME, FELLOW EXPLORERS, TO YOUR PERSONAL GUIDE THROUGH SAN FRANCISCO, CALIFORNIA.

When you sign your name here, you are making a commitment to two rules for this tour:

1. Have fun!
2. Be kind and respectful to the people and nature around you.

THIS SHRIMP 'N LOBSTER EXPLORATION BOOK BELONGS TO:

Look! A quote from a fellow city explorer!

I left my heart in San Francisco.

—a Tony Bennett CLASSIC!

As you explore any new place, you might feel a little bit out of your comfort zone. The best way to get comfortable? Ask questions!

WHAT TO PACK

The weather in San Francisco is infamous . . . for fog! It's so common that it has a name: Karl. (He even has his own Twitter account.) In fact, San Francisco summers (nicknamed "June Gloom") can be as chilly as the winters. The city is also unique for its microclimates: In a matter of a few short blocks, the weather can change from windy to warm. So be sure to prepare by wearing lots of layers. Try this: a T-shirt, a sweatshirt, a wind breaker, and a scarf.

Spring and fall are the best seasons to visit. Usually, that's when Karl takes a few weeks of vacation. No matter what, expect to do a lot of walking and have your comfortable shoes ready.

How could the weather be so chilly in a state with some of the best beaches in the country? We don't have the foggiest idea, but we've heard whispers about something called the Marine Layer.That's where the cold waters of the ocean and the hot summer air battle it out!

SAN FRANCISCO

Otherwise known as "The City by The Bay," San Francisco has also been called Gold Mountain, The Golden City, and even called "The Paris of the West." But think twice before you call it "San Fran" or "'Frisco." That won't go over well with the locals.

The oldest structure in town is a church known as Mission Dolores. Built in 1776 by the Spanish, it was originally called La Misión de Nuestro Padre San Francisco and is San Francisco's namesake!

San Francisco started out as a tiny town of 800 people. But thanks to the Gold Rush (1848–1855) and a long history of industrious entrepreneurs, the city has become one of the most sought after places to work and live in the United States.

HOW TO USE THIS BOOK

Read, learn, color, explore. Along with each of the interesting, fun, and exciting places to visit, we've included two sections: "Fascinating & True" and "Things to See & Do." We hope these will give you a deeper understanding of the history behind some of the people and places that make San Francisco special and get you actively involved in the people you meet. Now go explore!

THE MAP

Before beginning any journey, first check out a map. Do you see anything interesting? Cable cars, unique buildings, steep hills, lots of water, and even more fog. Just make sure you're ready for anything, because San Francisco is as unique as its weather.

The city stretches seven miles wide by seven miles long—pretty small compared to most major cities. So it may seem like it would be a snap to get around, but that's looking at it from a bird's-eye view. Since you're not a bird, you have to keep in mind those seven major (and steep!) hills that the early settlers first named—Nob Hill, Russian Hill, Twin Peaks, Mount Davidson, Telegraph Hill, Rincon Hill, and Mount Sutro.

N
W
E
S
New York City
Hawaii
Pacific Ocean
PRESID
US 1
LAKE STREET
SEA CLIFF
RODIN
LINCOLN PARK
RICHMOND DISTRICT
JAPANESE
TEA GARDEN
GOLDEN GATE PARK
MUSEUM
ACADEMY SCIENCES
SUNSET
DISTRICT
SAN FRANCISCO ZOO
LAKE MERCED
Ocean Beach
19th AVE.

San Francisco Bay
FISHERMANS WHARF
HYDE ST. PIER
ALCATRAZ
US 101
NORTH BEACH
CHINATOWN
TELEGRAPH HILL
Marina
COW HOLLOW
VAN NESS
RUSSIAN HILL
PACIFIC HEIGHTS
FINANCIAL DISTRICT
ORACLE PARK
I ♥ SF
NOB HILL
WESTERN ADDITION
YERBA BUENA
SOUTH BEACH
CIVIC CENTER
MARKET ST
US 80
HAYES VALLEY
ALAMO SQUARE
SOMA
MISSION BAY
HAIGHT ASHBURY
US 101
PROTRERO HILL
VALLEY
US 280
MISSION DISTRICT
DOG PATCH
NOE VALLEY
an Francisco

FERRY BUILDING
ONE FERRY BUILDING
Now that's an entrance!
It's the city by the bay, Shrimp!

This busy terminal is where crowds of commuters catch ferries to towns around the San Francisco Bay. It is also a major hub for foodies like us! Delight your senses by strolling through the many shops, including bakeries, restaurants, and gift stores that make it a world-class marketplace.

FASCINATING & TRUE

- ✓ The Ferry Building opened its doors in 1898 to serve the area's fast-growing fleet of ships, making it the second-busiest terminal in the world at the time.

- ✓ The showstopping, 245-foot-tall clock tower was inspired by the great Giralda Bell Tower in Seville, Spain. *Qué bonita! Vamos!*

- ✓ This structure is a survivor! It remained standing after both the 1906 and 1989 earthquakes.

THINGS TO SEE & DO

- Explore the Farmers' Market. Dig your pincers into the perfect produce that has made California's Central Valley famous for its fresh fruit and veggies. And to avoid getting crabby, quench those hunger pangs by choosing from a variety of gourmet food stands. Don't let the long lines deter you; this is one tasty spot well worth the wait.

- Take a day trip. Choose popular spots like Sausalito and Tiburon. Commute as they did during the Gold Rush. *All aboard!*

- Want to learn more about this historic building and foodie hot spot? Join a free walking tour. It will satisfy your taste buds and your historical curiosity.

THE EMBARCADERO

BETWEEN ORACLE PARK AND FISHERMAN'S WHARF

For some magnificent bay shore gazing, enjoy this three-mile-long walkway.

That's an art installation!
I ♥ SF

FASCINATING & TRUE

- ✓ "Embarcadero" is the Spanish word for pier and comes from the verb embarcar, meaning "go on board a ship." *We get it!*

- ✓ Before the construction of the Golden Gate and San Francisco–Oakland Bay Bridges, the piers handled 50 ferries—and up to 50,000 people—a day. *Now that's a seaworthy commute!*

- ✓ The enchanting Embarcadero took 46 years to complete, starting in 1878.

- ✓ The original shoreline was actually much further inland. Over time, it slowly moved east as the bay filled up with abandoned ships, landfill, and sediment.

THINGS TO SEE & DO

- Explore the city's public art pieces along the way; you can't miss Cupid's Span. This 60-foot bow-and-arrow—including feathers that quiver in the wind—was built by artists Claes Oldenburg and Coosje van Bruggen in 2002. Also look for the Crab Topiary (*our favorite, of course*) and Open Heart. *You'll love it!*

- Near Fisherman's Wharf, you'll see signs describing the local marine life. *Hey—that's us! Don't you think we should have a starring role?*

- Visit the end of Pier 7 for iconic views of the Bay Bridge. Stay for sunset, sit back, and watch the 25,000 twinkling lights dazzle in unison.

Look, Lobster! I can fit in this circle!
PLORATORIUM A COMMUNITY MUSEUM DEDIC
Shrimp! That's their sign. Let's explore what's inside!

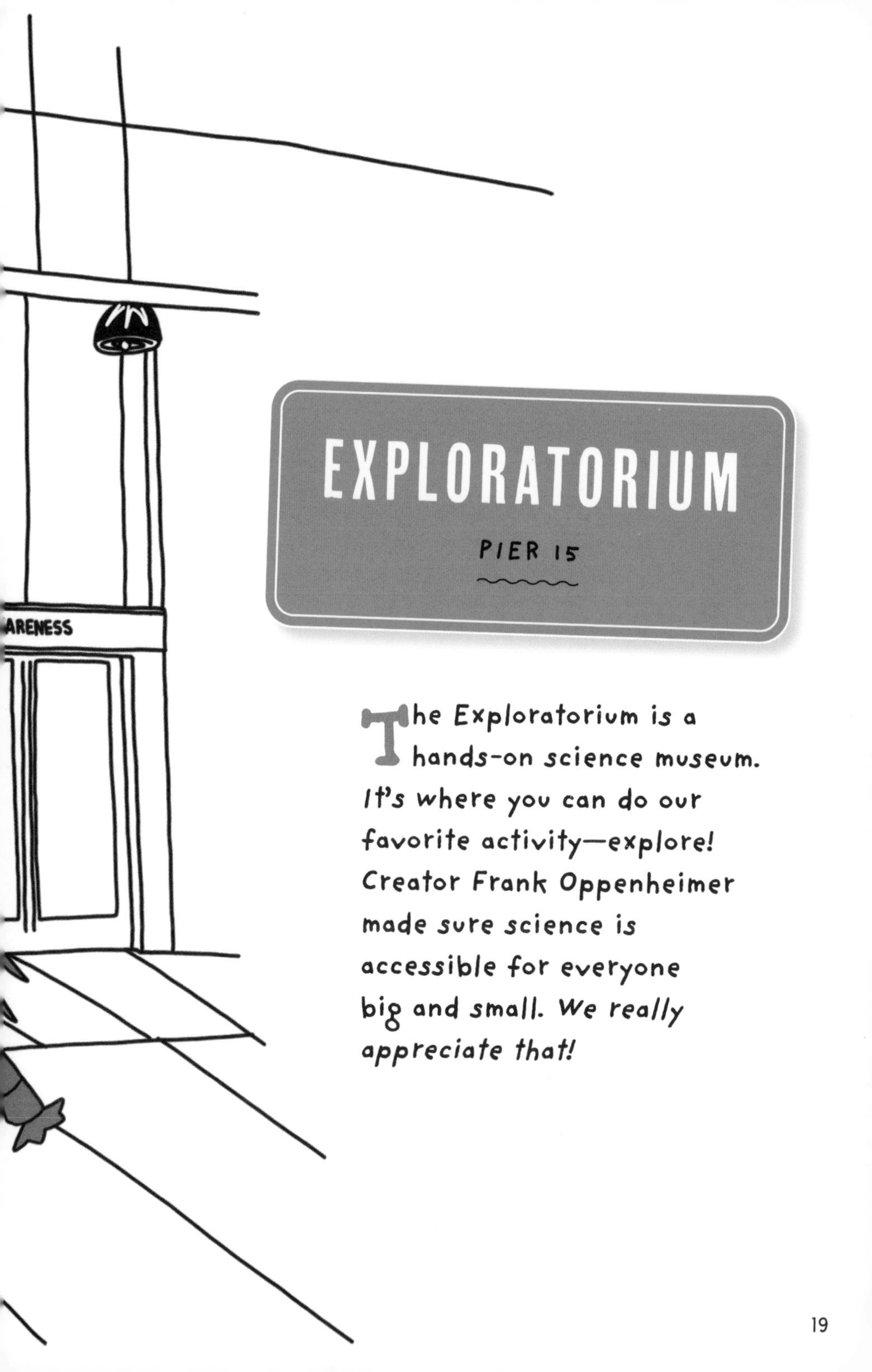

The Exploratorium is a hands-on science museum. It's where you can do our favorite activity—explore! Creator Frank Oppenheimer made sure science is accessible for everyone big and small. We really appreciate that!

FASCINATING & TRUE

- ✓ The Exploratorium was originally built in 1969 at the Palace of Fine Arts across town. In 2013, it moved to its present location along the waterfront.

- ✓ There is something for everyone: Six hundred fifty interactive experiments and lectures from the sciences, arts, technology, and outer space.

- ✓ You won't see the same museum twice. It's constantly growing and changing with new and exciting experiments and activities.

- ✓ Recognizing that the future is green, the Exploratorium is pushing to be the largest zero-net-energy museum in the world.

THINGS TO SEE & DO

- Want to experience being swallowed up in swirling fog? Check out the Tornado. It's not to be "mist!" Explore your inner Poseidon and control the waves of the Confused Sea. Have fun making crazy poses as you freeze your shadow in the Shadowbox Exhibit.

- You can engage in exhibits for FREE just outside the building. One of our favorites is the Archimedes Listening Vessels. There you can hold a conversation with someone 80 feet away . . . without YELLING.

ALCATRAZ

SAN FRANCISCO BAY

Welcome to the Rock. Convicts were housed in this prison from 1934 to 1963. It's a close 1.24 miles offshore, but the strong currents will challenge any boat . . . or even good swimmers like us. The ghostly buildings offer a grim reminder of life behind bars. A steady stream of ferries will shuttle you to this captivating spot. If you're on good behavior they'll also take you back!

FASCINATING & TRUE

- On August 12, 1775, Spanish explorer Manuel de Ayala discovered the island covered in pelicans, dubbing it "La Isla de los Alcatraces" (Island of the Pelicans). And that bird-brained phrase stuck!

- The prison staff and their families lived on the island in separate—safe!—quarters. They could enjoy a convenience store, bowling alley, dance hall, and gym. They probably had the first "cell" phones, too!

- Out of the 1,500 men imprisoned on the island, 36 dared to escape. Thirty-one were recaptured. The other 5 were never found.

THINGS TO SEE & DO

- Explore by day or night. By day you will guide yourself all over the island. By night, a guide will show you what made this jailhouse rock.

- Look for the cells of mob boss Al Capone, Machine Gun Kelly, and the "Birdman of Alcatraz," Robert Stroud.

- Check out Mother Nature! Alcatraz has a lot of birds. You might be lucky enough to spot the Brown Pelican that once thrived on this captivating island.

FISHERMAN'S WHARF

PIER 39

Fisherman's Wharf is a neighborhood that has always provided one thing that scares us: great seafood. And lots of it. The only difference between the 1800s and today is tourists. And lots of them!

PIER 39
PIER 39
Odoriferous. Pee-yew!
They are lazy.

FASCINATING & TRUE

- ✓ From modest stands selling clam chowder and shrimp cocktails (*Oh, no!*) during the Gold Rush, the neighborhood grew over time into the collection of restaurants we see today.

- ✓ Up to 12 million people visit the wharf every year, making it the #1 sight to see in San Francisco.

- ✓ Nobody knows why, but in 1990, a pod of sea lions decided to make the wharf their home. As many as 900 hang out in the summer near K-dock. You'll know they're there by their distinct sounds—and smells.

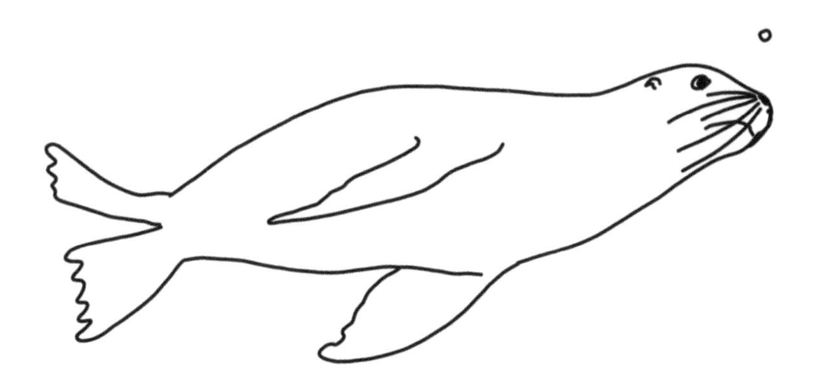

THINGS TO SEE & DO

- Visit the Aquarium of the Bay and explore local sea life through glass tunnels surrounded by 700,000 gallons of bay water. You can leave your scuba tank at home.

- Check out the Smartwater Stage—where you will be entertained by magicians, jugglers, musicians, and comedians—and the wonderful 2-level carousel.

- Step into the historic Musée Mécanique and experience an antique arcade from the 19th century. Bring some quarters because you've got 300 games to choose from!

- Jump on a sightseeing or whale-watching boat to get an amazing perspective of the Golden Gate Bridge and the crystal blue waters of the Farallon Islands.

HYDE STREET PIER

2905 HYDE STREET

This open-air museum allows you to experience what life was like at the turn of the 20th century. It harbors a tiny fleet of historic ships from the 1800s to launch your inner sailor. *Ahoy!*

FASCINATING & TRUE

✓ This historic pier was built in 1922 as a main terminal for the Golden Gate Ferry Company.

✓ Hyde Street Pier was once a part of US Routes 101 and 40. That all changed when the Golden Gate Bridge was built in 1937. All the cars took the bridge, and the ferry business was sunk.

✓ In the 1890s, the side-wheel paddle steamboat *Eureka* was a transporter ferry for up to 2,200 passengers and a handful of cars. *BEEP! BEEP!* Check out the vintage cars below deck.

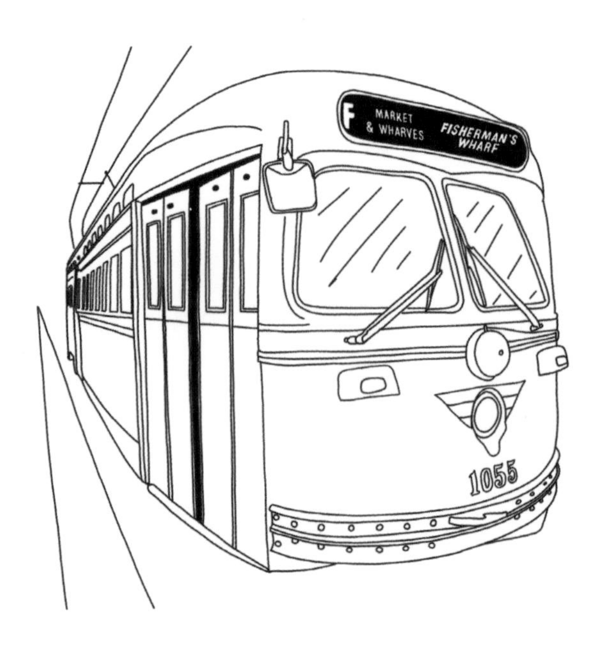

THINGS TO SEE & DO

- Exhibits at the Maritime Museum are fascinating—and free! Walk through the beginnings of this great harbor in the footsteps of early Native Americans. Then move into to the bustling industrial revolution of the mid-1800s and finally to the modern port we see today. You'll hear the sounds of an active harbor—from the elusive foghorn to sea lions, seagulls, and—*aarrrrghhh!*—sailors.

- Ships ahoy! Explore the grand vessels docked at the pier, including the Scottish-built *Balclutha*, which hauled grain, lumber, and salmon.

- Visit an early 1900s houseboat—we mean, Ark! Don't expect Noah and his gang to load up here. These living quarters were tight. . . . No room to march in two-by-two.

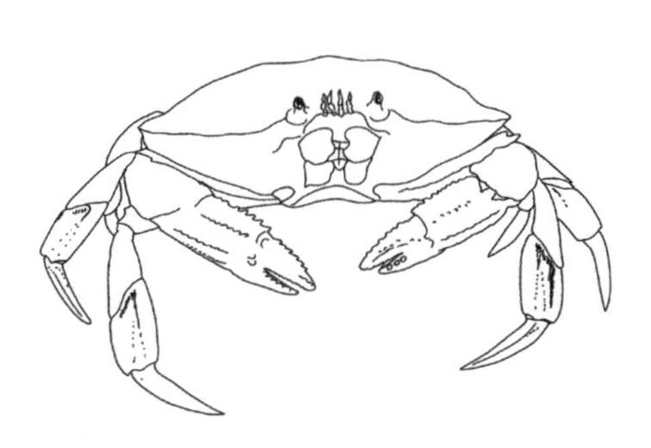

GHIRARDELLI CHOCOLATE COMPANY

900 NORTH POINT, SUITE 52

Ghirardelli Chocolate is the internationally celebrated chocolate company that ships its sweet confections all over the world to satisfy the cravings of chocoholics. It was started here in San Francisco in 1852, by Italian immigrant Domenico Ghirardelli.

FASCINATING & TRUE

- ✓ Ghirardelli was also an explorer . . . like us! He traveled to Uruguay, in South America, to learn about the chocolate and coffee businesses. After hearing about the Gold Rush, he packed up 600 pounds of his "chocolate gold" and set out for San Francisco to seek his fortune.

- ✓ The Ghirardelli Chocolate Company opened its doors in San Francisco in 1852—making it one of the oldest chocolate shops in the country; it also sold spices and mustards.

- ✓ The Ghirardelli chocolatiers found out that if they hung the processed cocoa in a warm room, the cocoa butter would drip out, leaving a richer-tasting chocolate. The result: that one-of-a-kind Ghirardelli taste. *How sweet it is!*

THINGS TO SEE & DO

- Visit the Ghirardelli shop and museum to learn how chocolate is made. Just don't expect to walk out with the recipe.

- It will be tough, but nobody will blame you if you decide to order a dessert. . . or two or three!

- Take a break at Ruth Asawa's mermaid fountain. It made a splash in 1968.

COIT MEMORIAL TOWER

1 TELEGRAPH HILL BOULEVARD

Set atop Telegraph Hill is the unforgettable Coit Tower. This 210-foot-tall tower was constructed in 1933 with funds donated by Lillie Hitchcock-Coit, a lifelong supporter of the local firemen. Upon her death, one-third of her estate was donated for the beautification of the city. Take the elevator up to the observation deck, and you'll leave your heart in San Francisco—just as she did.

FASCINATING & TRUE

✓ Telegraph Hill is named for the semaphore, a device for visual signaling, that once stood at its top. It informed the residents below of the kind of ships that were entering the harbor.

✓ Although Lillie Hitchcock-Coit was a huge supporter of the local firefighters, Coit Tower is not really designed to look like the nozzle on a fire hose as rumored. So you can put those flames to rest.

✓ The paintings on the interior walls of Coit Tower were funded by President Franklin Roosevelt's Public Works Administration, a project that helped support artists during the Great Depression in 1933.

THINGS TO SEE & DO

- Check out the murals by 25 different artists that decorate the inside of Coit Tower. It's free to enter, but it will cost you to take an elevator up to the observatory for those magnificent views. You'll quickly understand why it's the best spot in town—on a clear day—to see the boats sailing on the bay.

DESIGN YOUR OWN MURAL

LOMBARD STREET

BETWEEN JONES AND HYDE STREETS

This street wasn't designed to attract tourists; it's actually super-crooked for a technical reason. Lombard was built in 1922 with those eight hairpin turns to create a safer way for people to motor and walk the steep grade. Today, this charming brick-lined street with finely manicured gardens is one of San Francisco's favorite—and most photographed—landmarks.

I really think we should be on the sidewalk, Shrimp!
This is rad! I don't need to pedal!
DO NOT ENTER

FASCINATING & TRUE

- ✓ This one-way road stretches for over 600 feet, one block of winding, crazy curves.

- ✓ Two million people—plus us, if you're counting shellfish—visit this street every year. That's fun for the tourists but not always so much fun for some residents who have to carefully navigate getting in and out of their garages.

- ✓ Lombard is NOT the most crooked street in San Francisco. You'll have to head over to Vermont Street in the Potrero Hill neighborhood to find that.

COLOR IN YOUR VERY OWN LOMBARD STREET FLOWER BED.

THINGS TO SEE & DO

- This often congested, drone-attracting, super-selfie site might make you think a Hollywood film is in production. *Say "cheese!"*

- Join the crowd and drive or walk down Lombard to truly appreciate this wacky street.

- Enjoy the view while you're at the top and sort out your next stop. North Beach dead ahead.

- Be respectful to the neighbors and don't leave anything behind. After all, this is their front yard and you are their guests.

LEARN TO DRAW LOBSTER

DRAW BODY

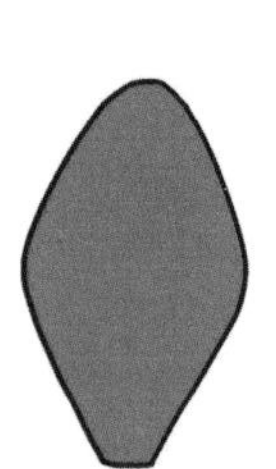

ADD ANTENNAE

ADD EYES

ADD PINCERS

ADD 4 LEGS

ADD TAIL

FINISH WITH MOUTH

NOW IT'S YOUR TURN

Okay, who added anchovies?
TONYS PIZZA

WASHINGTON SQUARE PARK

FILBERT STREET AND STOCKTON STREET

Welcome to Washington Square Park, the heart of North Beach. It's easy to spot, with the lofty steeples of the Church of Saints Peter and Paul jutting into the sky. Established in 1847, this park with its lush grass continues to charm residents and visitors like us. It's a haven within the busy city.

FASCINATING & TRUE

- The park is a registered landmark, all due to the gusto of the Telegraph Hill Dwellers, a neighborhood organization who got the state of California to recognize the park for its historic value. *Nothin's gonna change here!*

- Nearly 600 people lived in Washington Square Park for a year after the earthquake of 1906.

- Of the three original parks in San Francisco, Washington Square is the only one without a parking garage underneath it, unlike Union Square and Portsmouth Square in Chinatown.

- Saints Peter and Paul Church is known as "the Italian Cathedral of the West."

THINGS TO SEE & DO

- Have a picnic. It's a nice way to enjoy a little oasis in the middle of the hustle and bustle of the city.

- Look for the monument to the Volunteer Firemen of San Francisco. Like Coit Tower, it was financed by the socialite Lillie Hitchcock-Coit to honor her firefighting buddies.

DRAW THE PERFECT PICNIC

NORTH BEACH

BETWEEN BROADWAY AND HYDE STREET, COLUMBUS AVENUE AND THE EMBARCADERO

This neighborhood includes the Wharf, Little Italy, and parts of Chinatown. For years it was home to many aspiring writers, poets, and artists. Today, it continues to attract a diverse crowd while still holding on to its roots . . . you can smell it in the marinara cooking nearby.

FASCINATING & TRUE

- ✓ North Beach used to be . . . a beach! The original shoreline was located around Taylor and Francisco Streets. It was later filled in and built up during the late 1800s.

- ✓ Immigrants traveled here from all over the globe—South America, Europe, Australia—but it was the Italians who dominated the area in the mid-1800s—and still do.

- ✓ Filmmaker Francis Ford Coppola owns the 1907 Sentinel Building, also known as Columbus Tower. You can't miss it with its oxidized copper face and flat iron shape. Movies have been known to be made within those walls. *Lights! Camera! Action!*

THINGS TO SEE & DO

- Explore all the delicious cafes, shops, and restaurants. Surely there's a little piece of Italy for you to sink your teeth into. *Mangia!*

- Look up! On the corner of Columbus and Broadway is the "Language of the Birds" sculpture. This flock of flying books has dazzled unsuspecting visitors for more than a decade. Don't forget to look down: below your feet are the fallen words from the pages above.

- Walk around and listen, and you'll hear the sounds of Italy. Many people still speak Italian outside their shops and restaurants.

SAN FRANCISCO CABLE CAR MUSEUM

1201 MASON STREET

This museum, housed in the historic Washington/Mason cable barn and powerhouse, opened its doors to visitors in 1974. Exhibits explain how these wooden vehicles "rolled" the streets as the top mode of transportation for 30 years.

FASCINATING & TRUE

- ✓ Andrew Smith Hallidie built the first cable car in 1873. He created a pulley system with a continuously moving cable within a track. When the car grips the line, it is propelled forward. *Hang on!*

- ✓ The cable car's life almost came to an end after the 1906 earthquake, when many of the lines were destroyed. The streetcar became a better mode of transportation; soon after that, buses roared into action.

- ✓ Every year in October the city hosts a cable car bell-ringing contest in Union Square. The lighthearted competition started in 1949 and has become an annual tradition. *Now that's a tune we can listen to! Ding-ding!*

THINGS TO SEE & DO

- Go ride on a cable car! The boxy car will screech, vibrate, and cruise down some of San Francisco's steepest hills while giving you some of the best views of the Bay Area.

- Visit a cable car turntable at the end/beginning of the line and see how the gripman and conductor easily turn this 8-ton historic vessel.

DRAW A CABLE CAR

WELLS FARGO MUSEUM

420 MONTGOMERY STREET

This is no stagecoach parking garage . . . it's the Wells Fargo Museum. This exhibit showcases the origins of the Wells Fargo Stagecoach system and how it mastered long-distance bank and transportation services during the Gold Rush. Call it a midcentury Ferrari . . . no . . . Mustang! After all, six horses pulled the 2,500-pound vehicle on the rugged 2,812-mile Butterfield Overland Mail route—from California to Missouri—in just 25 days!

THINGS TO SEE & DO

- Check out the gold on display. This is the stuff that hundreds of thousands of dreamers hoped they would find in the rivers and hills—and what transformed San Francisco from a lowly cow town to a major metropolitan center. *Moo-ving on up!*

- Send a telegram. That's right, you can communicate with the other Wells Fargo branches using the telegraph system. It was the original email.

- Jump aboard a coach. See what it's like behind the horse-drawn wagons that traveled the West!

FASCINATING & TRUE

- Businessmen Henry Wells and William Fargo traveled from New York to San Francisco in the 1850s, joining the thousands who sought to get rich from the California Gold Rush and saw the need for this service.

- Along the route were more than 150 switch stations. These stations would allow weary horses and drivers to "switch out" a new team for the next stage of the journey (hence its name). But only a quick one. These stops were a short ten minutes.

- What ended the stagecoach? A faster means of transportation: the train. Once the Transcontinental Railroad was built in 1869, the stagecoach became a has-been and all services hit the rails. *CHOO-CHOO!*

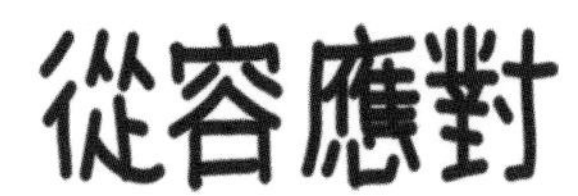

CHINATOWN

BETWEEN BROADWAY AND BUSH STREET, KEARNY AND POWELL STREETS

San Francisco's Chinatown is 24 square blocks of spice shops, vegetable stands, gift shops, and living quarters, making it one of the largest Chinese communities outside of China. Just get ready to be in a crowd—there are roughly 34,000 residents here.

I wonder if they make any that are organic and gluten free?
I smell COOKIES!
EN GATE
RTUNE
OKIE
CTORY
信念
看
幸福

FASCINATING & TRUE

- ✓ Portsmouth Square was the very first public square of San Francisco, built in 1846. It later became the heart of Chinatown.

- ✓ Grant Avenue marks the southern entrance to Chinatown and is one of its oldest streets. It is named after the Union Army General and later President Ulysses S. Grant. He lived in San Francisco, too.

- ✓ Chinese immigrants were the major labor force in the construction of the Transcontinental Railroad, linking the West to the East in 1869. The work was extremely dangerous and difficult, and cost many lives.

THINGS TO SEE & DO

- See if you can find the plaque in Portsmouth Square that marks the spot where the first American flag rose in San Francisco, claiming it as a United States territory, in 1846.

- Pass through the Dragon Gate. This entrance was built in 1969 as a gift from the Republic of China and is in the style of a traditional Chinese gateway.

- See how fortune cookies are made at the Golden Gate Fortune Cookie Factory. *Get 'em while they're hot!*

- Stay for the Chinese New Year parade. Since 1860 this annual tradition has featured the brilliant Golden Dragon. This mythical monster costume stretches 288 feet and requires a team of 100 people to move it through the streets—to keep it from draggin'!

YERBA BUENA GARDENS
750 HOWARD STREET
What do you think about heading East after this trip?
As long as exploring is involved, count me in!
URGE

A short distance from the heart of downtown, nestled among high-rises, museums, cafes, and restaurants, are the enchanting Yerba Buena Gardens. It is the perfect place to explore, relax, and learn. If you're lucky, you might even stumble upon an outdoor public concert. *Now that's music to our ears!*

Am I on this thing right?

FASCINATING & TRUE

✓ The Gardens of Yerba Buena—which means good herb—were named after a mint plant that grows in the area. Perhaps you'll get a whiff of it as you explore San Francisco!

✓ The Oche Wat Te Ou Reflection Garden pays tribute to the native Ohlone people who used to live in this area. There are stone pedestals for you to sit . . . and reflect.

✓ You can explore up to ten unique gardens for strolling and relaxing. Don't forget to stop and smell the roses.

✓ You are visiting the area commonly called SOMA—which stands for "South of Market Street." Back in the day, writer Jack London called this area "South of the Slot." The slot is where the famous cable cars grip the cable; and since the cable cars ran down Market Street, the nickname was born!

THINGS TO SEE & DO

- Listen for the gentle cascades of a serene waterfall. It will bring you to the Martin Luther King Jr. memorial. Hidden just past the falls is an enclosed walkway that is lined with inspirational quotes from this great hero.

- Explore the buzz and flutter around the Cho-En Butterfly Garden. Perhaps you'll find a new favorite. But leave those butterfly nets at home.

- The park also has learning days. Not only will you learn the seasonal life cycles of the gardens, but also you will pick up the best environmentally friendly practices to take care of Mother Nature.

- If you like to Ring-Around-the-Rosie, hop aboard the hundred-year-old LeRoy King Carousel. It was built in 1906. *Now you're getting around!*

- Swing by one of several museums, such as the Children's Creativity Museum. This eye-catching glass building offers hands-on learning through technology and the arts.

- Feeling like staying outside? The garden hosts outdoor plays and concerts to satisfy your inner thespian.

UNION SQUARE

BORDERED BY GEARY, POWELL, POST, AND STOCKTON STREET

Welcome to the square, where at every corner you will see high-end shops, art galleries, historic hotels, and the theater.

FASCINATING & TRUE

✓ Union Square earned its name from the Union Army supporters, who would rally in the park in the years leading up to and during the Civil War.

✓ Look up, and you'll see the Goddess of Victory as she stands atop the Dewey Monument. She was modeled after Alma de Bretteville, who married the wealthy owner of a sugar company, Adolph Spreckels. The results of their charity can be seen throughout the city. *Talk about a sweet family!*

✓ Guess what? You're standing on top of the world's first underground parking garage, built in 1941 in the United States.

CREATE A WINDOW DISPLAY FOR A FANCY SHOP

THINGS TO SEE & DO

- Check out the window displays in the fancy shops. They are always a hit, especially during the holidays, when the stores team up with local animal adoption agencies and fill their windows with adorable puppies and kittens.

- Feel like ice skating? During the holiday season the square hosts a skating rink. *We only have ice for you! Let's race!*

- Jump on a bus. This is a great way to go sightseeing!

- Just a few short blocks away is the theater district. Grab a matinee! In addition to the renowned American Conservatory Theater based here, shows also come straight from Broadway to dazzle your inner actor.

GRACE CATHEDRAL

1100 CALIFORNIA STREET

Taking up a full city block on the top of Nob Hill stands Grace Cathedral, the third-largest Episcopal cathedral in the country.

FASCINATING & TRUE

- ✓ The cathedral took 37 years to complete, from 1927 to 1964. A small construction delay . . . the Great Depression slowed things down a bit.

- ✓ If you want to see some classic Italian art, check out the bronze front doors called the "Gates of Paradise." They are an exact replica of the famed Ghiberti doors at the Baptistery in Florence, Italy. *Molto bello!*

- ✓ Just before his death in 1990, artist Keith Haring created a 600-pound altarpiece called "The Life of Christ." You can see it in the AIDS Interfaith Memorial Chapel.

COLOR THE STAINED GLASS WINDOWS

THINGS TO SEE & DO

- Check out the mazes. Look for the labyrinths both inside and outside the cathedral. On the second Friday of each month, the church hosts a mind-calming candlelight labyrinth walk with music.

- Take time to reflect on the 68 stained glass windows. See the Canticle of the Sun faceted glass rose window by Gabriel Loire of Chartres. Windows in the Human Endeavor series honor 20th-century pioneers including Albert Einstein and John Glenn. *They're definitely out of this world!*

- Grace Cathedral hosts countless events each year—from musical and dance performances to lectures and art exhibits . . . yoga anyone?

FAIRMONT HOTEL

950 MASON STREET

For more than 100 years, this luxury hotel has attracted the super-wealthy, big cheeses, and celebrities with rooms that feature some of the best views in the city. It is located in a neighborhood that was long-ago called Millionaires Row before it was destroyed by the great 1906 earthquake.

FASCINATING & TRUE

- ✓ Julia Morgan was the first woman to become a licensed architect in California. She designed and rebuilt the current Fairmont after it was devastated during the 1906 earthquake. It reopened in 1907.

- ✓ A steady stream of U.S. Presidents stayed at the Fairmont, leading it to be dubbed "the White House of the West Coast."

- ✓ Tony Bennett first sang "I Left My Heart in San Francisco" in the hotel's swanky Venetian Room.

- ✓ Today the Fairmont supports local honeybees with on-site hives. As a bonus, the Fairmont gets to keep the honey. *That's a sweet reward!*

- During the holidays, the Fairmont creates a life-size gingerbread house. It's 25 feet high, 35 feet wide, and 10.5 feet deep and features more than 6,000 gingerbread bricks. It's decorated with 1,650 pounds of candy and 3,300 pounds of royal icing. *Glad we packed our sweet tooth!*

- Enjoy Afternoon Tea. This is a favorite tradition at the hotel, enjoying tea and cakes and maybe a little of their honey! *Table for two, please!*

HERBST THEATER

401 VAN NESS AVENUE

The Herbst Theater is housed inside the War Memorial & Performing Arts Center. Completed in 1932 by famed architect Arthur Brown Jr., these chambers have treated audiences to the performing arts—from ballet to music. They continue to inspire and educate through lectures and events creating a special community all of its own.

FASCINATING & TRUE

- ✓ The Great Depression didn't keep theater buffs away from opening night at the War Memorial in 1932. The opera *Tosca* was completely sold out.

- ✓ This is the place where the United Nations was born! The charter was signed by President Harry Truman as well as delegates from fifty countries right on the stage of what is now the Herbst Theater on June 26, 1945. *That was quite a show!*

- ✓ The Japan Peace Treaty was signed here in 1951, reestablishing peace between Japan and the Allies at the end of World War II.

THINGS TO SEE & DO

- Check out a pre-performance lecture to get an in-depth understanding of the program.

- As you enter the theater, observe the Frank Brangwyn murals peeking between the columns. They were painted for the 1915 Panama-Pacific International Exposition.

- Check out special events! The ballet often hosts events to raise money for its educational programs.

PAINTED LADIES

STEINER AND HAYES STREETS

On the east side of Alamo Square, you will find a row of beautifully painted Victorian homes, the most photographed in the city!

FASCINATING & TRUE

- ✓ These homes can thank Elizabeth Pomada and Michael Larsen for their name. In 1978 the two wrote a book titled: *Painted Ladies—San Francisco's Resplendent Victorians.*

- ✓ Victorian homes were quickly fabricated during the Gold Rush. You could have any color you wanted as long as it was white! It wasn't until the 1960s that these buildings got their splashes of color.

- ✓ A Painted Lady has at least three different colors of paint that embellish all the fine details.

- ✓ Because the buildings are so photogenic, these streets have been dubbed Postcard Row.

COLOR THE PAINTED LADIES

THINGS TO SEE & DO

- Relax in the park and take in this quaint city neighborhood splashed with color.

- As you explore the city, see if you can spot more Painted Ladies. Though many of the houses no longer exist, tens of thousands were built over the late 1800s.

- Join the photo-op brigade. After all, this is Postcard Row!

DESIGN YOUR OWN PAINTED LADY

GOLDEN GATE PARK

BETWEEN STANYON STREET AND GREAT HIGHWAY, FULTON STREET AND LINCOLN WAY

Welcome to Golden Gate Park, 1,017 acres of former sand dunes that were transformed into forests, meadows, gardens, and lakes. A true escape for any city dweller.

FASCINATING & TRUE

- ✓ John McLaren, the park superintendent with a serious green thumb, introduced 600 new plant species to California.

- ✓ Golden Gate Park has been home to a herd of American bison since 1891, a tribute to the Wild West.

- ✓ Much of the park was created on uninhabitable areas that locals called the Outside Lands. The transformation began in 1871, after San Franciscans felt they needed a spacious public park.

- ✓ After the 1906 earthquake, 200,000 people temporarily made the park their home.

- ✓ Golden Gate Park hosts many free musical events, including the popular Hardly Strictly Bluegrass. *Don't forget your banjo!*

THINGS TO SEE & DO

- Take your time for a long walk in the park. You will learn to appreciate the microclimates as you head toward the beach. Stop at a museum or two along the way.

- Visit Stow Lake. You can walk around it or rent a boat and row across.

- Hike 430 feet up Strawberry Hill, the highest point in the park. Take a peek from the peak and enjoy the view of the park's first artificial waterfall, Huntington Falls.

- Explore the murals at the Beach Chalet building, which was built in 1925 as a changing room for beachgoers.

CALIFORNIA ACADEMY OF SCIENCES

55 MUSIC CONCOURSE DRIVE

Explore more than 400,000 square feet of exhibit space that includes an aquarium, planetarium, rainforests, a swamp, and an African Hall. One of the top attractions—besides the cute penguins—is Claude, the albino alligator. Maybe he'll smile for you as you enter.

FASCINATING & TRUE

✓ Cal Academy is one of the largest museums of natural history in the world and the oldest in California.

✓ It's also a research facility. The museum's in-house researchers and scientists continue to discover new species every year.

✓ The Morrison Planetarium is one of the largest digital domes in the world. Sit back and enjoy the show with 290 spectators. You'll never feel so small in such a large SPACE.

✓ The rolling hills of the "living" roof feature 1.7 million plants and flowers covering 2½ acres of rooftop. The unique looking skylights make the Academy a truly amazing sight.

THINGS TO SEE & DO

- Feel the humidity as you walk through the four-story Osher Rainforest, surrounded by butterflies, birds, and reptiles, too!

- Join a Penguins & Pajamas sleepover! You can snuggle up next to your favorite . . . Shrimp or Lobster.

- Tremble in the the Shake House as you experience the 7.9 quake of 1906 and the 6.9 tumbler of 1989. Hold on to your hats because the floor really moves!

JAPANESE TEA GARDEN

75 HAGIWARA TEA GARDEN DRIVE

This meditative oasis was created in 1894 by master gardener Makoto Hagiwara. Walk through the wooden gates at the Pagoda and cross the threshold to five acres of neatly manicured shrubs, calming streams and waterfalls, bridges and sculptures. Not one leaf is out of place— ESPECIALLY at the bonsai grove. This place is designed for your Zen and now.

FASCINATING & TRUE

- ✓ The Japanese Tea Garden was built for the California Midwinter International Exposition in 1894 to resemble a Japanese village.
- ✓ This "exhibit" was meant to be temporary but was so popular it became a permanent feature of Golden Gate Park.
- ✓ This is the oldest public Japanese garden in the United States.
- ✓ Drum Bridge was built in Japan and shipped to San Francisco in time for the Midwinter Exposition. You can't beat it!

THINGS TO SEE & DO

- [ ] Shhhh! Quiet yourself and sit in the garden, listen to nature.

- [ ] Have a cup of tea. After all, this is a Tea Garden.

- [ ] Walk around the gardens and appreciate the bonsai grove. *How old is that tree anyway?*

- [ ] Walk across—we mean climb up—Drum Bridge! *It's steep . . . but fun!*

OCEAN BEACH

FROM CLIFF HOUSE TO FORT FUNSTON

This long stretch of beach will take you from the Cliff House all the way to the zoo . . . stretching more than three miles along the brisk Northern California coast.

FASCINATING & TRUE

✓ Ocean Beach has been the site of many shipwrecks. The treacherous currents and frequently fogged-in jagged coastline have made it a historically dangerous spot for ships.

✓ The waves at Ocean Beach have attracted surfers from around the world. But beware! Powerful sneaker waves have taken people by surprise, dragging them out into the ocean. This is one place you don't turn your back on.

THINGS TO SEE & DO

- At low tide, look for the remains of the clipper ship *King Philip* that wrecked in 1878. It's one of many that went under the powerful spell of strong currents... and a heavy fog. *KARL!*

- Look around at Mother Nature. You might find yourself face to face with a rare western snowy plover, a shy bird that winters in the area. Or perhaps you'll find curious sea lions frolicking in the waves. They like to surf, too!

- Tour the ruins of the Sutro Baths, near the former Cliff House. Once an escape for San Franciscans, the baths could accommodate 10,000 people at once. Built in 1894, the building burned down in a June 1966 fire.

LEGION OF HONOR

100 34TH AVENUE

Opened in 1924, this grand and historic museum is full of Egyptian and Roman artifacts and paintings by Monet, Renoir, and Rembrandt.

FASCINATING & TRUE

✓ The museum was a gift to San Francisco from Alma de Bretteville Spreckels and her husband, the sugar company heir Adolph Spreckels. Remember them from Union Square? They aimed to beautify the city with art and culture, and this museum was their memorial to the Californians who died during World War I.

✓ The Legion of Honor was modeled after the 18th-century Palais de la Légion d'Honneur in Paris—only this palace is three-fourths the size of the original. *Voila!*

✓ Alma's friendship with French sculptor Auguste Rodin and her love of art led her to buy 13 of his sculptures for the museum. She continued to collect 90 pieces of his art, until her death in 1968.

THINGS TO SEE & DO

- Hold on to your ticket—it will also get you into the de Young Museum in Golden Gate Park.

- See if you can spot Rodin's famous *Thinker* sculpture. *Hmmmmm. We thought you could!*

- Bring your sketchbook and activate your inner artist!

- Listen . . . to the organist who plays the famous Spreckels Skinner Organ on weekends.

With lush trees, neatly manicured lawns, and military barracks that have been converted into popular office space and housing, the Presidio feels like the countryside within the city limits.

FASCINATING & TRUE

- ✓ The Presidio was established as a Spanish outpost in 1776 and became a U.S. Army base in 1848. It served a major role in the defense of the west coast during World War II.

- ✓ The wetlands are a habitat for nearly 200 species of birds. *Grab your binoculars!*

- ✓ In 2005, George Lucas built Lucasfilm's primary headquarters on the site of a decommissioned Army hospital. Today it's also home to the special effects division, Industrial Light & Magic.

THINGS TO SEE & DO

- Visit the Walt Disney Family Museum and learn about Walt Disney and the creation of the magical Disney empire.

- Look for the Yoda Fountain. Outside the ILM headquarters building. *Find it you will.*

- Tour Fort Point. Located below the Golden Gate Bridge, the fort was home to 500 men and 102 cannons protecting the city from possible invaders during the Civil War.

PALACE OF FINE ARTS

3601 LYON STREET

The Palace of Fine Arts was meant to be a temporary structure, built by architect Bernard Maybeck, for the Panama-Pacific International Exposition in 1915. The success of the Exposition put the city back on the map as a true destination spot after the devastating earthquake and fire of 1906.

FASCINATING & TRUE

✓ At the end of the world's fair, preservationists saved the Palace from demolition in order to honor its beauty and stature.

✓ In 1964, the Palace was torn down and rebuilt with stronger, longer-lasting material to withstand earthquakes.

✓ To the right and left of the dome you'll notice additional columns topped with statues of weeping women, their mournful faces hidden. The architect wanted to express a sense of sadness at all the devastation.

THINGS TO SEE & DO

- Look out for the pair of swans, a couple of the Palace's favorite residents.

- Find the 20-foot angel sculptures in the dome's rotunda. Hint! They will be looking down at you.

- Sing a tune. Stand in the center of the dome and listen to your voice echo throughout the rotunda.

San Francisco's most famous structure is the 1.7-mile-long bridge called the Golden Gate. It's been wowing onlookers since its completion in 1937.

GOLDEN GATE BRIDGE

AT FORT POINT, SAN FRANCISCO,
CROSSING TO LIME POINT, SAUSALITO

FASCINATING & TRUE

✓ The Golden Gate Bridge is named after the strait that it crosses where the San Francisco Bay meets the Pacific Ocean.

✓ President Franklin Roosevelt took part in the opening ceremonies . . . well, sort of. From Washington, D.C., he pushed a telegraph key that officially opened the bridge for business. Beep Beep! Pedestrians had first dibs to walk over the day before, officially opening the bridge on May 27, 1937.

✓ In 1987, on the occasion of the Golden Gate's 50th birthday, the city hosted another bridge walk, closing access to vehicles. Nearly 300,000 pedestrians joined the festivities, weighing down the arch of the bridge by seven feet. Don't worry . . . it bounced back. Just as it was designed to do.

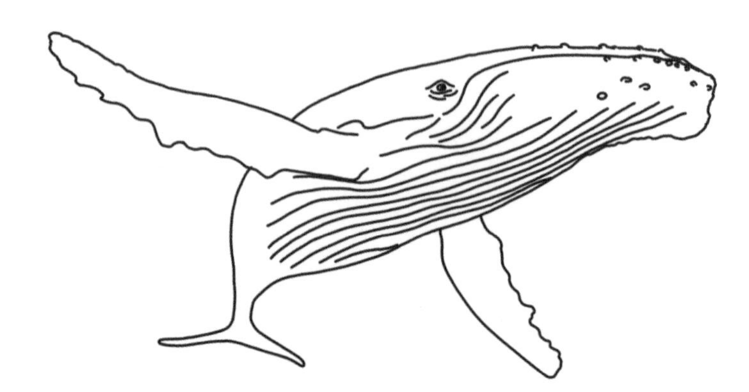

THINGS TO SEE & DO

- Bundle up and take a walk. Just know that pedestrians walk on the east side of the bridge while bikers take the west.

- While on the bridge, see if you can spot any ocean creatures. Marine life like dolphins and whales have been known to come into the bay. *Thar she blows!*

- Vista Point on the north end of the bridge is a primo spot for shots of the city before you start the 1.7 mile walk back.

ANGEL ISLAND

SAN FRANCISCO BAY

This California State Park is a short ferry ride from San Francisco and is a local favorite for long days of picnicking, hiking, and biking. It's a haven for outdoor enthusiasts as well as history buffs. Join the 200,000 people a year who visit the "Ellis Island of the West" and learn about what has been called the gateway to Gold Mountain.

FASCINATING & TRUE

- In 1910, the island became an immigration and quarantine station for newly arrived immigrants. Before closing in 1940, more than one million immigrants passed through.

- In 1970, a park ranger found Chinese poetry etched in the wall describing the experience of being confined on the island.

THINGS TO SEE & DO

- Visit the Immigration Station. This historical museum displays stories and photos.

- Bring your tent, sleeping bag, and cooler. Camp under the stars . . . or in the fog!

- Take a hike! Visit historic sites along the way. Want to go big? Summit Mt. Livermore and be dazzled by 360-degree views of the Bay!

- Jump on a Segway tour or tram! You'll roll through the island with an audio tour to "tune" into its historic past.

- Had enough? Board the ferry to Tiburon and check out the Arks, houseboats from the 1890s that have been transformed into shops!

Wow, what a trip! What did you think about our adventure to San Francisco? Was there anything you found to be super interesting? What most impressed you? Most surprised you? We saw and did so much, it's sometimes hard to remember everything. Good thing you've got this guide to help out! Now you can easily revisit your adventure with us. And guess what? You can use what you learned to lead your own expedition in the future. How cool is that? Knowing where you're going is a lot of fun!

LIST THE PLACES YOU'D LIKE TO SEE IN SAN FRANCISCO:

1

2

3

4

5

HERE ARE A FEW OF OUR FAVORITES!

Visit Coit Tower and look for the famous wild parrots on Telegraph Hill. Say hello to the sea lions at Fisherman's Wharf. Ride a bike across the Golden Gate Bridge. *Wheeee!*

We love exploring with you, and we can't wait to go on another great adventure. In fact, we were so inspired by the *Thinker* at the Legion of Honor, we're "thinking" about visiting other cities. Would you like to join us?

Your salty bffs,

Shrimp 'n Lobster

ACKNOWLEDGMENTS

This series would not be possible without the support and guidance of Angela Engel and her rock stars at the Collective Book Studio, pun master and mentor Jeff Myers, my dear friend Sharon Fox, and most importantly my parents who set me on the path to get out there and see the world. Mah, this journey is for you.

ABOUT THE AUTHOR

Charlotte Rygh's passion for exploring the oceans provides inspiration for her unique illustrations. She is a graduate of the Kanbar Institute of Film and Television at NYU's Tisch School of the Arts, and she currently calls the San Francisco Bay Area her home. To Learn more about Charlotte's work, and her two favorite crustaceans, visit shrimpnlobster.com.